# NATURE'S WRATH
## THE SCIENCE BEHIND NATURAL DISASTERS

# THE SCIENCE OF
# TORNADOES

MATT ANNISS

Gareth Stevens
Publishing

Please visit our website, www.garethstevens.com. For a free color catalog of all our high-quality books, call toll free 1-800-542-2595 or fax 1-877-542-2596.

Library of Congress Cataloging-in-Publication Data

Anniss, Matt.
 The science of tornadoes / Matt Anniss.
     p. cm. — (Nature's wrath : the science behind natural disasters)
 ISBN 978-1-4339-8664-2 (pbk.)
 ISBN 978-1-4339-8665-9 (6-pack)
 ISBN 978-1-4339-8663-5 (library binding)
 1. Tornadoes.  I. Title.
 QC955.A58 2013
 551.55'3—dc23

                                    2012023548

First Edition

Published in 2013 by
**Gareth Stevens Publishing**
111 East 14th Street, Suite 349
New York, NY 10003

© 2013 Gareth Stevens Publishing

Produced by Calcium, www.calciumcreative.co.uk
Designed by Simon Borrough and Nick Leggett
Edited by Sarah Eason and Vicky Egan
Picture research by Susannah Jayes

Photo credits: Cover: Top: Shutterstock: Todd Shoemake; Bottom (l to r): Dreamstime: Dustine; Shutterstock: Alexey Stiop; Dreamstime: James Bushelle; Shutterstock: Daniel Loretto; Dreamstime: Pancaketom. Inside: Dreamstime: James Bushelle 6tr, Dustine 24cl, Pancaketom 38cr, David M. Schrader 28tr, Christopher White 43bl, Lisa F. Young 42cl; FEMA: Jace Anderson 36cl, 36-37tc; FEMA News Photo: Andrea Booher 1cr, 13, 14, 15cr; FEMA Photo: Tim Burkitt 34c; Flickr: Sean Waugh NOAA/NSSL 8c; NASA: Image courtesy The GOES Project Science Team 35tl; NOAA: NWS 16tr; Shutterstock: Guido Amrein, Switzerland 17, Marcel Baumgartner 32l, Melissa Brandes 45cr, Shae Cardenas 38cl, ChameleonsEye 39c, DarkOne 11cr, Dustie 4c, 18cl, 23bl, 24r, 25cr, Dvande 43tr, EmiliaUngur 1cl, 7, EPG_EuroPhotoGraphics 31tl, Judy Kennamer 18-19t, Daniel Loretto 5b, 10c, 21l, 41, Map Resources 30c, R. Gino Santa Maria 29, 37cl, MaxyM 20cl, Melanie Metz 27t, Todd Shoemake 45tl, Alexey Stiop 31b, John Wollwerth 9c; Wikipedia: Tyler Arbogast 40tr, US Army Corps of Engineers (Kansas City) 23cl, United States' National Weather Service (NWS)/Redrawn by Renata3 26cl.

Printed in the United States of America

CPSIA compliance information: Batch #CW13GS: For further information contact Gareth Stevens, New York, New York at 1-800-542-2595.

# CONTENTS

# WHAT IS A TORNADO?

A tornado is one of the most destructive natural events on Earth. Every year, thousands of buildings are damaged or destroyed by tornadoes. Plants, trees, signposts, and buildings go flying in every direction as these giant funnels of wind sweep across the land.

With wind speeds sometimes reaching hundreds of miles an hour, tornadoes can destroy homes in a matter of seconds.

## Stormy Weather

A tornado is a spinning column of air that forms during extreme storms. Most tornadoes look like a funnel. The funnel shape extends downward from a thundercloud until it touches the ground. The air in the funnel moves in a circular motion, creating a giant column of violent wind. In the most extreme tornadoes, wind speeds can reach an amazing 300 miles (480 km) per hour.

## Size and Speed

The size of a tornado depends on the width of the part of the funnel that touches the ground. In some cases the funnel is only several feet wide, in others it can be up to 330 feet (100 m), and can travel between 5 and 100 miles (8 and 160 km) before dying out.

## Where do Tornadoes Occur?

Tornadoes have been seen on every continent except Antarctica. However, they are most common in the Great Plains of the United States, from Texas in the south to the Dakotas in the north. About 1,200 tornadoes occur here every year.

### WORLD'S WORST

The deadliest tornado on record struck Bangladesh on April 26, 1989. The tornado quickly moved for 50 miles (80 km) through the cities of Daulatpur and Salturia, destroying buildings and uprooting trees. It is estimated that the 1-mile (1.6 km) wide tornado killed about 1,300 people. About 12,000 others were injured and 80,000 people lost their homes.

Millions of people whose homes are in the Great Plains region of the United States are at risk of a tornado strike.

# CHAPTER ONE

# THE SCIENCE OF TORNADOES

The first sign that a tornado is on its way is when a funnel-shaped column of air sweeps down from a storm cloud toward the ground. When the funnel makes contact with the ground, it becomes a tornado. After "touchdown," the tornado can last for several minutes or even hours. The route that the tornado takes across the ground is known as its "path."

This photograph shows the damage that a tornado can do to homes and backyards that lie directly in its path.

## TORNADO STRUCTURES

The few people who have seen the inside of a tornado say that the middle, known as the "eye," is very calm with no wind at all. It is also extremely dark inside the eye. At the outer edges of the tornado, the air circulates at up to 300 miles (480 km) per hour. It rotates counterclockwise in the United States and other Northern Hemisphere countries, and clockwise in the Southern Hemisphere. Eventually, the funnels of rotating air become as thin as rope, and the tornadoes blow themselves out.

### WORLD'S WORST

In November 1915, a tornado hit Great Bend, Kansas, ripping up trees and lifting fences, roof tiles, and other objects high into the air. Many of these objects later "rained down" more than 80 miles (130 km) away. A sack of flour from one farm was found around 110 miles (180 km) from Great Bend!

When a tornado hits a building, pieces of wood, concrete, and roof tiles may be whirled hundreds of feet into the air before they fall back down to the ground many miles away.

7

# HOW DO TORNADOES FORM?

Most tornadoes form in the middle of an extreme thunderstorm known as a "supercell." They happen when warm, moist air becomes trapped between a layer of cold, dry air above and a layer of warm, moist air below. The warm, moist air rises and punches through the layer of cold air. As the warm air spirals upward, winds at different levels make it spin faster. This area of constantly circulating air is known as a "mesocyclone."

If you look carefully at this supercell storm cloud, you can see a funnel cloud beginning to form at the back. This area of cloud looks a little like a curving arrow.

## A Rotating Cloud

As rainfall within the thunderstorm increases, it drags down an area of quickly descending air, called a downdraft. The downdraft speeds up as it approaches the ground, and drags the mesocyclone toward the ground with it. As the mesocyclone nears the ground, a funnel cloud descends from the base of the storm. When the funnel touches the ground, it becomes a tornado, also known as a "twister." It then increases in speed and power as it feeds on the warmer surface air.

## Hitting the Ground

The tornado's rotating air at ground level can be so violent, and its wind speeds so great, that anything in its path is destroyed. Powerful tornadoes such as this are incredibly destructive. However, only 1 percent of tornadoes are powerful. Most tornadoes are weak and cause only minor damage to the areas they travel across.

In this supercell storm, the clouds are clearly moving in a circular direction, a sure sign of the mesocyclone above.

## The Right Conditions

Although there are many thousands of tornadoes around the world every year, they are still a relatively rare event. This is because only certain thunderstorms produce the supercell clouds needed for a mesocyclone to form. Even then, scientists believe that only 20 percent of supercell storms actually produce tornadoes.

# VORTEXES, SPOUTS, AND DUST DEVILS

Tornadoes come in many shapes and sizes. While some are big enough to destroy entire buildings and send cars flying into the air, others are so small that people barely even notice them. On very rare occasions, a tornado may form with two to five funnels, or "spouts." This spectacular type of tornado is known as a "multiple-vortex tornado."

## Multiple Tornadoes

Sometimes, one violent thunderstorm can produce a series of tornadoes, known as a "tornado family." The funnels usually travel in a parallel line, but sometimes their paths overlap. When lots of tornadoes hit the same area in a short space of time, the destruction can be particularly bad.

Here, a trio of funnel clouds have formed from the same storm. When they touch down they will become a rare multiple-vortex tornado.

## Landspouts and Waterspouts

In some areas, weak tornadoes named "landspouts" are common. Landspouts have a smooth, tubelike shape. They form when winds, swirling at ground level, are sucked upward into an updraft of air. As the swirling air stretches upward, it spins even faster until it finally reaches the clouds. When this type of funnel forms over water, it is known as a "waterspout."

Waterspouts can regularly be seen sweeping across the seas around the Florida Keys, as well as over many lakes in the United States.

## WORLD'S WORST

Waterspouts form fairly frequently, but are rarely deadly. The deadliest waterspout on record took place in the Grand Harbor of Valletta, on the island of Malta, in 1551. An entire fleet of ships was destroyed, leaving 600 sailors dead.

## Dust Devils

A dust devil is a spinning column of wind, into which dust and dirt become caught up, making it visible. Dust devils form when the weather is hot and dry, with light winds. The hot air near the ground quickly rises through the cooler air above. As the air rises, it spins into a long, thin column that looks like a tornado. Dust devils are particularly common in Arizona.

# BRIDGE CREEK—MOORE, 1999

Bridge Creek and the city of Moore are located in the heart of the Midwest.

Bridge Creek and Moore

Oklahoma, in the Midwest, is no stranger to tornadoes, but few expected the wave of destruction that hit the state on the night of May 3, 1999. In just over 90 minutes, a single, violent tornado killed 36 people, injured 583, and damaged over 8,132 homes. By the time the tornado finally blew itself out at 7:48 p.m., it had caused more than $1.4 billion worth of damage across the region.

Along with his two terrified children, Tom Tinneman was hiding in the closet of his trailer when the tornado hit Bridge Creek:

"The house started to tremble, and I felt the tie downs break loose on one side of the trailer. We started to roll over. It was like the tornado picked the whole home up and threw it down again."

**Survivors Speak**

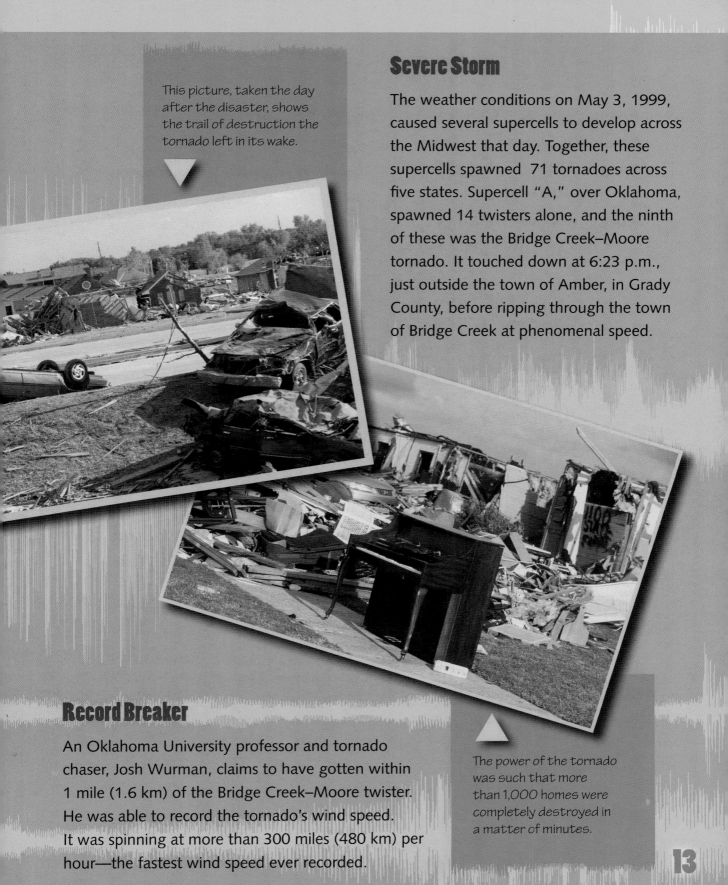

## Severe Storm

The weather conditions on May 3, 1999, caused several supercells to develop across the Midwest that day. Together, these supercells spawned 71 tornadoes across five states. Supercell "A," over Oklahoma, spawned 14 twisters alone, and the ninth of these was the Bridge Creek–Moore tornado. It touched down at 6:23 p.m., just outside the town of Amber, in Grady County, before ripping through the town of Bridge Creek at phenomenal speed.

This picture, taken the day after the disaster, shows the trail of destruction the tornado left in its wake.

The power of the tornado was such that more than 1,000 homes were completely destroyed in a matter of minutes.

## Record Breaker

An Oklahoma University professor and tornado chaser, Josh Wurman, claims to have gotten within 1 mile (1.6 km) of the Bridge Creek–Moore twister. He was able to record the tornado's wind speed. It was spinning at more than 300 miles (480 km) per hour—the fastest wind speed ever recorded.

# SUPER DESTROYER

In Bridge Creek, two houses were completely destroyed, leaving nothing more than a bare slab of concrete where they had once stood. On the street, a layer of asphalt was torn from the surface.

## Path of Destruction

From Bridge Creek, the tornado quickly moved on to the city of Moore, before reaching the Oklahoma City limits. At one point, hundreds of cars were tossed into the air as the tornado sped down a highway.

In Oklahoma City, many residents found their homes reduced to piles of rubble.

In this iconic image of the disaster, a lone US flag flutters amid scenes of utter devastation.

## The Bridge Creek–Moore Tornado, 1999

**MAY 3, 1999**
**3:30 p.m.**
A massive supercell thunderstorm forms over Tillman County in Oklahoma.

**4:15 p.m.**
The Storm Prediction Center issues a severe storm warning for the southwestern part of Oklahoma.

**4:51 p.m.**
The first of 14 tornadoes formed in supercell "A" touches the ground on the highway Route 62.

**6:23 p.m.**
The ninth tornado from supercell "A" touches down just southwest of Amber in Grady County.

**6:27 p.m.**
The tornado quickly intensifies and hits the town of Bridge Creek. Two houses there are completely destroyed.

**6:57 p.m.**
The first-ever tornado emergency alert is issued for the Oklahoma City Metro area.

**7:20 p.m.**
The tornado again intensifies as it passes through the city of Moore.

**7:30 p.m.**
The tornado crosses into Oklahoma County and soon begins to batter the southern fringes of Oklahoma City.

## The Aftermath

The Bridge Creek–Moore tornado was one of the most destructive twisters of recent years. The amount of death, destruction, and injury it caused highlighted how badly prepared Oklahoma was for a major tornado. In the 10 years that followed, over 6,000 reinforced "storm rooms" were installed in homes across the state.

**Samantha Darnell quickly took shelter with her husband and baby when she realized the tornado was approaching her home:**

"It sounded huge—a beast! I heard the windows being shattered and the floorboards splinter. It sounded like the house was being torn apart."

As the tornado swept through the region, people had to dodge falling trees and dangerous pieces of flying debris.

**7:48 p.m.**
The tornado finally blows itself out just outside of Midwest City.

**MAY 4, 1999**
President Bill Clinton declares a state of disaster in 11 counties in Oklahoma. The American Red Cross opens 10 shelters to house 1,600 people.

**MAY 5, 1999**
Aid donations pour in from across the United States.

**MAY 7, 1999**
Nearly 1,000 members of the Oklahoma National Guard are sent to the region to assist with the recovery. A search for 13 still missing people continues.

**MAY 8, 1999**
A disaster recovery center is opened in the city of Moore.

**MAY 12, 1999**
Seven clean-up teams start the process of removing debris, including smashed cars, fallen trees, and bricks, timber, and roofs from wrecked homes.

**MAY 21, 1999**
Local officials announce that over 3,000 volunteers from around the United States have traveled to the area to help assist with the huge clean-up operation.

# CHAPTER TWO

# STUDYING TORNADOES

Although there have been many scientific breakthroughs in recent years, there are still many things we do not understand about why tornadoes form in particular supercell storms. Thankfully, it's now easier to predict where and when tornadoes may touch down. Satellite pictures beamed from space show the movement of cloud formations and weather patterns, making tornadoes easier to predict.

## RADAR AID

Scientists use specially designed equipment called Doppler radar, better known as weather radar. In the United States, a network of radar stations across the country helps scientists to track storms as they develop. Radar stations can detect the development of rotating, "cyclonic," winds inside storms from more than 100 miles (160 km) away. This data is shown as a map on a computer screen in a monitoring station, such as the Storm Prediction Center in Oklahoma. Areas of the radar map that appear red, orange, or pink are supercell thunderstorms, which may soon spawn potentially dangerous tornadoes.

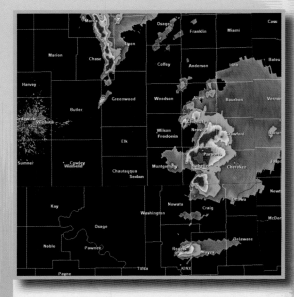

The red, orange, and pink areas on this satellite radar image show the location of dangerous supercell storms likely to produce tornadoes.

## WORLD'S WORST

A supercell storm is an alarming sight for weather forecasters, but even more worrying is a hurricane. This is an extremely severe and large storm, sometimes hundreds or even thousands of miles wide. In 2004, Hurricane Ivan moved across the Caribbean and United States, causing billions of dollars worth of damage. Ivan spawned 117 tornadoes, which is still a world record today!

Technology has revolutionized our understanding of tornadoes. Doppler radar and satellite imagery make it easier than ever to predict tornado strikes.

# MEASURING TORNADOES

If you were to stand in the path of an oncoming tornado to try to measure its speed, you would be swept off your feet and very likely killed. So, how do scientists accurately measure the strength of tornadoes? To overcome the problem of recording accurate wind speeds, in 1971 a scientist named Tetsuya Fujita designed a method by which tornado damage could be analyzed. It was named the Fujita Scale (later renamed the Enhanced Fujita Scale).

These houses were hit by a tornado measuring "F5" on the Fujita Scale.

A tornado measuring only "F1" on the Fujita Scale can still cause significant damage to buildings. This church was hit by an "F1" tornado.

## Rating Tornadoes

Fujita's idea was simple. He believed that scientists should look carefully at the damage done by tornadoes to property, trees, and plants. He said that scientists should also examine weather radar images and the markings left on the ground by tornadoes. By doing so, Fujita believed scientists could accurately rate the strength of any tornado on a sliding scale.

Although devastating tornadoes are most common in the United States, they do sometimes occur in Europe. On April 9, 2012, a powerful tornado laid waste to a construction site in Elazig Province, Turkey. The tornado left a 6.8-mile (11 km) path of destruction, with six people dead and many others injured.

## Using the Scale

Ever since Fujita's findings, scientists have used the Fujita Scale to rate tornado strength. The weakest tornadoes, those with an estimated wind speed of less than 70 miles (112 km) per hour are rated as "F0." At the other end of the scale, extremely violent tornadoes are classed as "F5." These tornadoes have wind speeds upward of 260 miles (418 km) per hour and are capable of causing the most incredible damage.

The giant Bridge Creek–Moore tornado that ripped through Oklahoma in 1999 was one of the most extreme "F5" tornadoes ever recorded.

# TORNADO SEASON

If weather conditions are right, tornadoes can strike almost anywhere in the world, at any time of day or night. Scientists have discovered a number of factors that make tornadoes more likely. One of the biggest factors is climate—how warm or cool an area is, and how much humidity is in the air. In certain parts of the world, the climate changes at certain times a year, becoming hot and moist. These conditions are perfect for tornado formation, and it is at these times that twisters are most likely to strike.

Farmers in the Midwest know that when their spring crops are fully grown, the tornado season is not far away.

## Perfect Tornado Weather

In the United States, tornadoes occur most frequently during spring (April to June) and fall (September and October). At these times of year, the air is likely to be moderately warm and moist, making tornado-spawning storms more likely. Elsewhere in the world, similar climate conditions are found at other times of the year. In Germany, for instance, tornadoes are most likely to occur in July.

A tornado's path begins when its funnel touches the ground and ends when it dies out. The longest-ever tornado path was the Tri-State Tornado of 1925. The tornado traveled for 218 miles (350 km) through Missouri, Illinois, and Indiana.

## Magic Time

Not only do tornadoes occur during certain weather patterns, but they are also more likely to take place at certain times of the day. Scientists have discovered that most tornadoes in the United States happen in the afternoon and early evening, between 3:00 p.m. and 7:00 p.m. Within this window, there is one particular hour at which tornadoes are most likely to strike—research suggests that people are most likely to see a tornado at 5:00 p.m. People call this the "five o'clock magic!"

Scientists have discovered that tornadoes are much more likely to occur as the sun begins to set.

Joplin, Missouri

Joplin is located in a region where the threat of twisters is a daily concern.

Joplin, Missouri, is a sleepy city in the heart of "Tornado Alley." Over the years, it has been hit by several strong tornadoes, and now has its own tornado warning sirens. When the sirens went off at 5:11 p.m. on Sunday, May 22, 2011, the city's residents knew what to expect, but what followed was worse than they ever could have imagined.

## Touch Down

Less than 20 minutes later, a strong tornado touched down near the Kansas state line. It quickly grew to become one of the most catastrophic tornadoes on record. At one point, its path was more than 1 mile (1.6 km) wide. Over the next hour, the tornado swept through Joplin, flattening everything in its path. It tore down buildings and crushed entire areas. The local hospital of St. John's was badly damaged and some reports state that the building was moved 4 inches (10 cm) off its foundations.

"It's just gone. We heard the tornado sirens for the second time. All of a sudden, everything came crashing down on us. We pulled our heads up and there was nothing. It was gone."

**Survivors Speak**

## Neighborhoods of Dust

On Main Street and 20th and 26th Streets, every building was damaged or flattened to the ground. Trees were stripped of their bark, or simply swept away. A nursing home for the elderly was completely destroyed, and a number of nearby schools were badly damaged. As the tornado neared a restaurant, the manager herded his staff and customers into a walk-in freezer. He held the door shut against the tornado until he was swept up into it, where he died.

JOPLIN MISSOURI TORNADO PATH IMPACTED AREA

Legend

Structure Damage

Location Map

This map shows the 2011 tornado's catastrophic path of destruction through the heart of Joplin.

Many Joplin residents had to sift through the remains of their homes to find cherished family possessions.

# FULL IMPACT

Many stores and restaurants in the worst-hit areas of Joplin were flattened to the ground. Large pieces of concrete and sizeable trucks were picked up from the ground by the tornado and hurled into the air. Some vehicles and large objects were hurled some distance away from the place where they were picked up. Many houses were simply lifted up off their foundations, carried away, and then dumped in shattered pieces on the ground.

A young girl surveys the wreckage of a once-familiar Joplin neighborhood.

## The Joplin Tornado Strikes, 2011

**MAY 22, 2011, 5:11 p.m.**
After hearing that a tornado is imminent, Jasper County Emergency Operations Center sounds Joplin's emergency warning sirens for the first time that day.

**5:17 p.m.**
The National Weather Service sends out warning signals to weather radio handsets.

**5:31 p.m.**
The warning sirens sound for a second time in Joplin.

**5:34 p.m.**
The tornado touches down near the end of 32nd Street, Joplin, close to the Kansas state line.

**5:41 p.m.**
The tornado gathers in strength as it hits a densely populated area to the south of the town. Part of the hospital is destroyed.

**6:00 p.m.**
Joplin High School is destroyed. Luckily no one was in the building at the time.

**6:10 p.m.**
A Walmart store is severely damaged and several restaurants, including a Pizza Hut, are flattened.

## The Cost of the Damage

By the time the tornado left Joplin, it had destroyed over 7,000 buildings—roughly 20 percent of the city. In the process, 161 people had lost their lives. It was the single most deadly tornado in the United States since the late 1940s. It was also the costliest. In the days after the tornado, the damage to the city was assessed and it was estimated that the worst-hit parts of the city would cost more than $3 billion to rebuild.

The insurance claims to homes, cars, and other property after the Joplin disaster ran into millions of dollars.

The devastation caused by the tornado was so severe that diggers had to be used to clear the wreckage.

**6:12 p.m.**
The tornado finally begins to die out.

**7:00 p.m.**
Missouri Governor Jay Nixon declares a state of emergency for the Joplin area and orders in extra emergency response teams.

**MAY 23, 2011**
Nearly 400 extra state troopers, national guards, and marines help with the search and rescue operation.

**JULY 15, 2011**
By this time, there have been 16,656 insurance claims.

**Local newspaper journalist Jeff Lehr was sitting in his bedroom when the huge tornado hit Joplin:**

"There was a loud huffing noise and my windows started popping. I had to get downstairs as glass was flying everywhere. I opened a closet and pulled myself into it. Then you could hear everything go. It tore the roof off my house. I came outside and there was nothing left."

**Survivors Speak**

25

# PREDICTING TORNADOES

Weather radar, satellite images, and complicated computer programs allow scientists to predict where tornadoes may occur. However, many ordinary people still rely on traditional methods of storm and tornado "spotting" to keep them safe from danger. Since the 1970s, the US government has run a revolutionary program named Skywarn to teach people the art of storm spotting.

Some storm chasers are willing to take dangerous risks in order to film tornadoes close up.

Skywarn's many volunteer storm spotters play a key role in the defense against tornadoes.

## Spotting Tornadoes

At present, there are over 230,000 trained Skywarn storm spotters in the United States. Skywarn spotters are taught the difference between supercell storm clouds (those that are most likely to spawn tornadoes) and regular storm clouds. They are told to look at the rear end of a supercell storm cloud. If the rear is rain-free, the conditions are right for tornado formation.

As the storm builds, a rotating wall of cloud may descend from the main storm cloud, forming the shape of a curving arrow. Storm spotters are trained to notify the emergency services at once if they see this, because it's a sure sign that a tornado is on the way. It generally takes between 5 and 30 minutes for the cloud to spiral down and touch the ground.

## Storm Chasing

Some people want to do more than simply spot extreme storms and warn of their approach. They also want to follow the path of such storms, and get as close to the action as they can. The highlight for them is to see a tornado touch down, and to follow its path. "Storm chasers," as they are known, often record their adventures on film. Storm chasing was the subject of the 1996 hit movie, *Twister*.

# CHAPTER THREE

# TORNADOES AND THE UNITED STATES

The United States is the most tornado-prone place on Earth. Every year, about 1,200 tornadoes touch down on US ground—more than in any other country on the planet. While many of these hit remote, rural areas, some rip through towns and cities causing billions of dollars worth of damage.

## UNDER ATTACK

People in the United States have always lived in fear of deadly tornadoes. The first recorded tornado in the United States was in Reheboth, Massachusetts, in August 1671. Nine years later, another tornado hit Cambridge, Massachusetts, leaving one person dead. Since then, many more people have died or lost their homes as a result of tornadoes. On average, 81 people die each year in tornado strikes, and 1,500 more are injured. Tornadoes have been recorded in every state in the United States, including Alaska in the far north and Hawaii in the Pacific Ocean. They are, however, most common in the states of Texas, Oklahoma, and Florida.

Storm chasers capture incredible pictures of supercells while driving on highways across tornado-prone states.

### WORLD'S DEADLIEST

The Tri-State Tornado of 1925 holds a number of records. As well as featuring the longest continuous path, it was also the deadliest in US history. In total, 695 people died, which swept through three southern states in just two devastating hours.

Clearing up after a tornado is a familiar ritual for the residents of many US states, particularly in the South and Midwest.

# TORNADO ALLEY

Although tornadoes have been spotted in every American state, they are most likely to appear in an area of the country known as "Tornado Alley." Here, the threat of destructive tornadoes is greater than anywhere else in the world.

The area in orange shows the location of Tornado Alley, where tornadoes are most likely to strike.

## Storm Center

Tornado Alley is a popular term associated with the states that lie between the Rocky Mountains to the west and the Appalachian Mountains to the east. These two mountain ranges run the entire length of the United States, north to south. Within Tornado Alley, the most frequent tornado outbreaks occur in northern Texas, Kansas, and Oklahoma. Florida also has high numbers of tornadoes, but they are usually less severe in strength.

## WORLD'S LUCKIEST

If a person becomes caught in the path of a tornado, it is unlikely that they will live to tell the tale. Matt Suter of Fordland, Missouri, is one of the rare exceptions to this rule. In March 2006, he was swept off his feet by a tornado and carried 1,305 feet (398 m). Amazingly, when the tornado dropped him, he was able to get up and walk away!

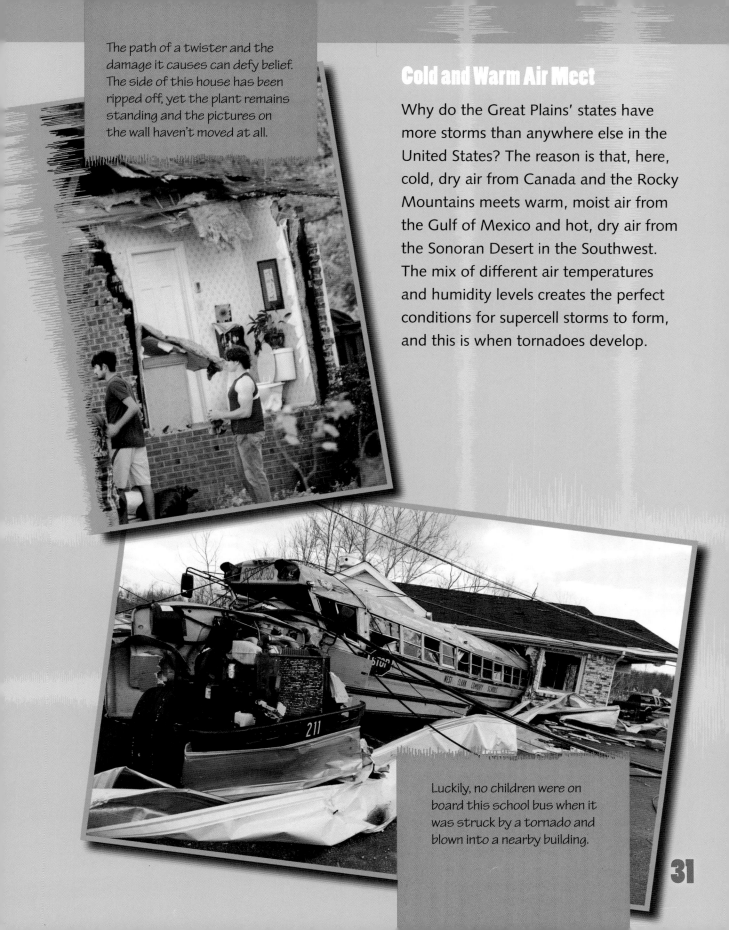

The path of a twister and the damage it causes can defy belief. The side of this house has been ripped off, yet the plant remains standing and the pictures on the wall haven't moved at all.

## Cold and Warm Air Meet

Why do the Great Plains' states have more storms than anywhere else in the United States? The reason is that, here, cold, dry air from Canada and the Rocky Mountains meets warm, moist air from the Gulf of Mexico and hot, dry air from the Sonoran Desert in the Southwest. The mix of different air temperatures and humidity levels creates the perfect conditions for supercell storms to form, and this is when tornadoes develop.

Luckily, no children were on board this school bus when it was struck by a tornado and blown into a nearby building.

# AROUND THE WORLD

**Although the United States is the most tornado-ravaged country on Earth, other places in the world are also frequently hit by tornadoes. From the Netherlands and Russia to Bangladesh and Pakistan, deadly tornadoes can touch down anywhere, destroying everything in their paths.**

Tornadoes and dust devils, such as this one, are especially common on the Ladakh Plains of India.

## WORLD'S WORST

One of the deadliest tornado events in Europe took place in Italy on September 11, 1970. An outbreak of tornadoes swept through the Veneto region in the north, causing a huge amount of damage to towns and cities, including Venice. In total, 36 people died.

## Hitting Bangladesh

Three of the ten most deadly tornadoes of all time have hit the poverty-stricken country of Bangladesh in southern Asia. As well as the record-breaking tornado of 1989, which left 1,300 people dead, 923 people died following a strong tornado in 1969. Then, in 1973, the village of Balurchar was completely destroyed and eight other villages were all but destroyed, leaving 686 people dead.

## Throughout Asia

In Southeast Asia, tornadoes have caused severe damage in the Philippines and Malaysia. In June 2010, 120 people were injured when a tornado swept through the Malaysian city of Petaling Jaya. Frightened survivors said that the tornado's force was enough to blow the roof completely off an apartment block.

Tornadoes have been reported on every continent except Antarctica. In 2011, there were more than 100 tornadoes in Europe and several disastrous events in Southeast Asia.

Mykanow, Poland

Canada

North America

USA

Europe

Asia

Venice, Italy

Bangladesh

Africa

Philippines

South America

South Africa

Petaling Jaya, Malaysia

Australia

New Zealand

## From Africa to Canada

Tornadoes have also been spotted in South Africa, Australia, New Zealand, and Canada. Canada is one of the only places in the world where scientists have seen a "winter waterspout." This is a tornado over water created by a heavy snowstorm.

In Europe, about 500 tornadoes take place every year, but few of them are particularly strong or deadly. However, every so often, a serious outbreak will hit a country and make headlines. In August 2008, three people died when eight tornadoes ripped through Mykanow, Poland.

# REAL-LIFE SCIENCE
# SUPER OUTBREAK, 2011

In April 1974, an outbreak of 148 tornadoes left a trail of damage, death, and destruction across 13 American states. It became known as the "super outbreak." This two-day deadly tornado onslaught left hundreds of people dead. Many residents thought they would never see such devastation again. Sadly, they were wrong.

This satellite image shows a massive storm formation similar to the one that caused the 2011 "super outbreak." The storm clouds cover much of the eastern United States.

## Stark Warning

On April 19, 2011, the Storm Prediction Center in Oklahoma put out a severe storm warning. Forecasters had calculated that many southern states would be engulfed by one of the most extreme thunderstorms ever seen. The message was clear—between April 25–28, expect the worst.

In the days following the 2011 "super outbreak," the extent of the damage across the United States became clear. It was one of the worst natural disasters in US history.

34

**Kirk Green lost his brother Charlie and his good friend Jamie, a mother of three children, when their mobile home was hit by a tornado in Georgia:**

"Jamie was very brave. She could have jumped ship, but she stayed with Charlie. The biggest tragedy of this whole thing is that she had three young children. I feel extremely sad for those children that they're not going to be able to grow up knowing their mom."

## Violent Storms

The first tornado touched down on the afternoon of April 25. Over the next three days, most of the states in the South, Midwest, and Northeast were battered by severe storms, flooding, and an almost endless stream of violent tornadoes. To begin with, the tornadoes were weak and scattered over a large area. By the evening of April 25, the storms had intensified and were causing serious damage to a number of towns in Arkansas. Tornadoes destroyed parts of the Little Rock Air Force Base, damaging three airplanes and more than 100 houses.

By April 27, many states were preparing for the prospect of truly catastrophic tornadoes. Mississippi was particularly badly hit. One tornado measuring "F4" on the Fujita Scale swept away a number of homes, tossed cars in the air, and scorched a 6.5-feet (2 m) deep path into the earth near the town of Philadelphia. As the day progressed, "F5" tornadoes ripped across the states of Mississippi and Alabama. Less severe twisters were also reported in Georgia, Tennessee, Arkansas, Virginia, and as far north as New York State.

# MONSTER TORNADO

By the time the storm finally cleared Florida on April 29, the United States had experienced its worst tornado outbreak of all time. In total, a staggering 358 tornadoes touched down across 21 states in those four days. These included four "F5" tornadoes in one day. This was a highly abnormal occurrence—the United States usually sees just one "F5" a year.

Homes were crushed under the weight of falling trees and other debris during the 2011 super outbreak.

The tornado that struck this house wasn't one of the strongest, but it was still severe enough to cause extensive damage.

## The Outbreak Commences

**APRIL 19, 2011**
The Storm Prediction Center issues a warning for April 25–28, 2011, saying that severe storms are likely to affect a wide area of the country.

**APRIL 25, 2011**
**3:00 p.m.**
The first tornadoes are spotted in the southern states of Oklahoma and Texas.

**3:25 p.m.**
The Storm Prediction Center issues a "particularly dangerous situation" tornado watch for Arkansas, Missouri, Texas, and Louisiana.

**6:00 p.m.**
A tornado emergency is declared for Vilonia, Arkansas. Later, an "F2" tornado hits, destroying 80 homes.

**7:00 p.m.**
An "F3" tornado sweeps through Hot Springs Village, Arkansas. One person is killed and homes are destroyed.

**8:00 p.m.**
A tornado destroys part of Little Rock Air Force Base, Arkansas.

**APRIL 26, 2011**
The Storm Prediction Center says there is a "high risk" of severe weather for parts of Louisiana, Arkansas, Oklahoma, and Texas. Supercell storm clouds in Michigan lead to tornado warnings. Weak tornadoes hit Texas, Louisiana, and Arkansas. An "F3" tornado hits Fort Campbell, Kentucky.

## Number of Dead

Some 322 people died across six states, including 235 in Alabama alone, as a result of the storms. Thousands of homes were destroyed or damaged. A few days later, one government official estimated that the cost of rebuilding stricken communities would run to more than $11 billion.

Baptist Pastor Mike Hornsby rode out the tornado outbreak by hiding in the bathroom of his house. When it was over, he found his house had been blown nearly 200 feet (60 m) to the east by a savage twister:

"We could feel it up in the air, feel it moving. It felt like the house was coming apart."

After the storm had passed, thousands of families across the United States looked on in disbelief at the ruined remains of their homes.

**APRIL 27, 2011 AFTERNOON**
An "F5" tornado touches down in Mississippi, causing incredible damage to Philadelphia. Three more "F5" tornadoes hit towns in Alabama.

**3:00 p.m.**
A multi-vortex "F4" tornado in Cullman, Alabama, damages 867 homes.

**4:00 p.m.**
In Lawrence County, Alabama, 24 people die as a very strong tornado rips through.

**5:10 p.m.**
A hugely destructive tornado ravages Tuscaloosa, Alabama, killing 44 people. It then moves on to destroy parts of the northern suburbs of Birmingham.

**EVENING**
A supercell storm and several tornadoes damage northern Virginia, Maryland, and Pennsylvania.

**APRIL 28, 2011**
249 tornado deaths are reported in 48 hours in Alabama. The last 24 hours sees 260 tornadoes reported, setting a new record.

More tornadoes hit Pennsylvania, New York, Virginia, North Carolina, South Carolina, Florida, and Maryland. An "F3" tornado strikes Glade Spring, Georgia.

**APRIL 29, 2011**
The storm finally begins to break. For the first time in four days, no tornadoes are reported.

# SAVING LIVES

For people living in many parts of the United States, especially those in Tornado Alley, the threat of tornadoes is a very real one. Many people have friends and relatives whose homes have been destroyed and their lives ruined by tornadoes. It is for this reason that many precautions are taken to protect people and property against tornado strikes in this threatened part of the United States.

Storm shelters are built below ground, away from buildings that may collapse, in order to make them as safe as possible.

Public storm shelters are increasingly common in parts of the United States particularly vulnerable to tornado strikes.

STORM SHELTER

## WORLD'S WORST

Many people think that tornadoes affect only rural areas, but this is not true. Many cities have been devastated by tornado strikes. In 1953, 114 people died when a massive "F5" tornado hit Waco, Texas. Nearly 600 people were injured.

## Listen Up

If the Storm Prediction Center and National Weather Service think a tornado strike is imminent, they will issue warnings. These are sent to all local radio and television stations in the areas likely to be affected. In some US states, a warning siren will also sound.

## Rural Warnings

People on farms or in rural areas do not have the benefit of warning sirens, but they can buy their own weather radio to listen out for warnings. This is a portable device that flashes storm and tornado warnings on a digital display. As soon as people know a tornado is on the way, they immediately head for cover.

## Storm Shelters

During a tornado, the best place to be is in a storm shelter or cellar. This is a specially built, pre-fab shelter sunk into a hole in the ground. It is designed to withstand the force of an "F5" tornado. Storm shelters and cellars are very common in tornado zones.

After a tornado hits, the frantic search for people trapped in buildings begins.

## Taking Shelter

People who do not have a storm shelter or cellar are advised to take cover in a first floor interior area, such as a bathroom or closet. An unused mattress offers protection from flying debris. If a person is outdoors when the tornado approaches, they should shelter as deep underground as possible. Survivors of tornadoes have hidden in ditches or large drainpipes.

# CHAPTER FOUR

# THE FIGHT AGAINST TORNADOES

Until the early 1950s, the only warning people had of an approaching tornado was seeing it in the distance. Today, very few tornadoes appear without warning. Scientists with special knowledge of the weather are known as meteorologists. They study weather patterns, radar readings, and other data to predict what the weather will be in the coming days and months.

The Storm Prediction Center in Oklahoma provides the National Weather Service with early warnings of supercell storms.

## SCIENTISTS AT WORK

In the United States, the organization that compiles weather forecasts is the National Weather Service. The section dedicated to spotting storms and the likelihood of tornadoes is the Storm Prediction Center in Oklahoma. Here, scientists look out for storms that could produce tornadoes 24 hours a day. First, the Center tells local National Weather Service offices that a bad storm is likely. When a supercell storm forms, they issue a "tornado watch." This tells people that a tornado will probably occur in the next 6 hours. If a tornado has formed, or is likely to occur in the next hour, an urgent tornado warning is sent out.

### WORLD'S WORST

The most destructive tornado ever to take place solely on Canadian ground happened in July 1987. In an event known locally as "Black Friday," a strong "F4" tornado destroyed parts of the city of Edmonton, Alberta. Hundreds of people were injured and 27 people died.

By the time a big tornado such as this one touches down, the National Weather Service will already have sent out an urgent warning notice.

# ONE STEP AHEAD

Since the 1970s, a number of technological and scientific developments have helped meteorologists to understand more about storms and tornadoes. They are able to give more accurate predictions of when and where storms are likely to occur, and this has helped people to stay one step ahead in the fight to save lives.

Scientists use technology such as radar systems to predict where tornadoes will hit.

## Radar Vision

The most important breakthrough in predicting tornadoes was the development of a system called Doppler radar. Based on radar systems used by the military, Doppler radar stations send and receive electronic signals. Doppler radar systems can detect how much water there is in the air, and therefore how likely rainfall is.

**WORLD'S WORST**

Residents of Auckland, New Zealand, were surprised by a tornado on May 3, 2011. After touching down at around 3:00 p.m., the tornado swiftly moved through the area, leaving behind a 3-mile (5 km) trail of destruction. One person died and 14 were injured.

## Computer Predictions

Data received by Doppler radar stations is fed into a computer. Using an advanced piece of software, scientists are able to use this data to predict accurately the size, shape, location, type, and movement of storms. From this information, computerized weather maps are created that show the accurate location of storms.

## Hooking Tornadoes

In 1973, it was found that tornado-producing supercell storms show up on radar images in a particular way. They look like a hook and are called "hook echoes." Whenever a hook echo appears on a computerized weather map created from radar readings, scientists know that a tornado is forming. No one knows exactly how many lives have been saved because of the development of Doppler radar, but is likely to be in the millions.

Doppler radar towers, such as this one, are found across the United States. They help scientists to keep track of severe thunderstorms.

Doppler radars have helped scientists to accurately pinpoint the location of tornadoes before they even touch down.

# A YOUNG SCIENCE

Over the last 50 years, our knowledge of how and why tornadoes form has increased greatly. However, there are still some things scientists do not understand, so they are constantly working to find out more. They know how thunderstorms form and the climate conditions that create supercell formations, but do not yet fully understand why certain supercell clouds begin the process, called "tornadogenesis," that spawns tornadoes.

## WORLD'S LUCKIEST

In 1991, a television news crew and several other people successfully survived a tornado near Andover, Kansas, by hiding under a highway overpass. They were incredibly lucky. Studies show that highway overpasses are one of the worst places to take shelter. People are more likely to get injured there than survive the onslaught.

Many years ago people believed that dust devils were tornadoes. Today, our understanding of these natural phenomenons has dramatically improved.

## Perfecting the System

Doppler radar has allowed scientists to predict areas where tornadoes are likely to form, and even touch down. However, they cannot yet predict how intense a tornado will be or how long it will last. If one day scientists perfect a system to accurately predict a tornado's strength and projected path, even more lives could be saved.

Mobile Doppler radar devices attached to cars and trucks are helping scientists get closer than ever to tornadoes, helping them to work out exactly what happens inside them.

Tornadoes are one of nature's most unpredictable events. However, with improved technology, it will be possible to predict them more quickly and reduce their devastating effects.

## On the Move

One project that is helping our understanding of how tornadoes behave is Doppler On Wheels. This is a fleet of three trucks mounted with Doppler radar receivers. Since they were introduced, the trucks have been able to observe nearly 150 tornadoes up close. Research projects such as these will continue for many years to come as we carry on the endless fight against tornadoes, one of nature's most extreme events.

45

# GLOSSARY

**circulating:** moving around continuously in circles

**debris:** the remains of anything broken or destroyed

**formation:** how something forms or comes together. Also used to describe something once it has come together.

**foundation:** the concrete base of a building upon which the rest is built

**funnel:** a tube or pipe that is wide at one end and narrow at the other, with an opening at each end

**humidity:** a scientific term for measuring how much moisture (water) there is in the air

**imminent:** about to happen

**install:** put into something

**Northern Hemisphere:** the half of the earth that is north of the equator, an imaginary line around the middle of the planet, at equal distance from the Poles. The United States, Canada, and Europe are in the Northern Hemisphere.

**portable:** small enough to be carried easily in a pocket or bag

**precaution:** to take steps to stop something bad from happening

**predict:** to make a guess that something will happen in the future based on knowledge

**project:** to show what will happen in the future

**prone:** likely to happen

**reinforce:** strengthen

**remote:** far away

**rural:** in the countryside rather than in a town.

**state of emergency:** a crisis situation within a country. All normal local or national government business is suspended so that officials can concentrate on resolving the crisis.

**stricken:** badly damaged

**Veneto region:** the area around the city of Venice in northern Italy

**vortex:** a whirling mass of air. No tornado can form without a vortex first occurring inside a storm cloud.

# FOR MORE INFORMATION

## Books

Adamson, Heather. *Surviving a Tornado*. Mankato, MN: Amicus Readers, 2012.

Dougherty, Terri. *The Worst Tornadoes of All Time*. Mankato, MN: Capstone Press, 2012.

Gonzales, Doreen. *Tornadoes*. New York, NY: PowerKids Press, 2013.

Mogil, H. Michael and Barbara G. Levine. *Extreme Weather*. New York, NY: Simon & Schuster Books for Young Readers, 2011.

## Websites

Find out more about tornadoes and how they form.
**kidsknowit.com/interactive-educational-movies/free-online-movies. php?movie=Tornadoes**

Discover tornadoes and their many varying types and features.
**theweatherchannelkids.com/weather-ed/weather-encyclopedia/tornadoes/ types-of-tornadoes**

Discover lots more about tornadoes.
**weatherwizkids.com/weather-tornado.htm**

# INDEX

## A
Alabama 28, 35, 37
Arizona 11
Arkansas 28, 35, 36

## B
Bangladesh 5, 32, 33

## C
Canada 31, 33, 40

## D
Dakotas 5
Doppler Radar 16, 17, 42, 43, 44, 45
dust devils 10, 11, 32, 44

## E
emergencies 14, 24, 25, 26, 36
Enhanced Fujita Scale 18
eye (of tornado) 6

## F
Florida 11, 28, 30, 36, 37
"F5" tornados 18, 19, 35, 36, 37, 38, 39
Fujita Scale 18, 19, 35
Fujita, Tetsuya 18
funnels 4, 5, 6, 8, 10, 11, 21

## G
Georgia 35, 37
Germany 20

## I
Illinois 9, 21
Indiana 21

## K
Kansas 6, 22, 24, 27, 28, 30, 44
Kentucky 28, 36

## L
landspouts 11

## M
Malta 11
Maryland 37
mesocyclones 8, 9
Mississippi 28, 35, 37
Missouri 21, 22, 23, 24, 25, 30, 36
multiple-vortex tornados 10

## N
National Weather Service 24, 38, 40, 41
New York State 35, 37
North Carolina 37

## O
Oklahoma 12, 13, 14, 15, 16, 19, 30, 34, 36, 40

## P
Pennsylvania 37

## R
radars 16, 18, 26, 40, 42, 43, 44, 45
radar maps 16

## S
satellite images/pictures 16, 17, 26
Skywarn 26
South Carolina 37
storm chasers 26, 27, 28
Storm Prediction Center 14, 16, 34, 36, 38, 40
storm shelter 15, 38, 39
storm spotters 26
supercells 8, 9, 13, 14, 16, 26, 28, 31, 36, 37, 40, 43, 44

## T
Tennessee 28, 35
Texas 5, 30, 36, 38
Tornado Alley 22, 30, 38
tornadogenesis 44

## V
Virginia 35, 37

## W
waterspouts 11, 33
wind speeds 4, 9, 13, 18, 19